INSIGHT GUIDES

Instant
alaska

APA PUBLICATIONS

Part of the Langenscheidt Publishing Group

L

CONTENTS

Compiled by Pam Barrett

Photography by Alaska Division of
Tourism; Alaska Resources Library and
Information; Alaska State Library; Alaska
Travel Industry Association; Anchorage
Convention and Visitors Bureau; Tom
Bartel; Bernholz & Graham Public
Relations; Fairbanks Convention and
Visitors Bureau; Gary Heger / Skagway
Convention and Visitors Bureau; Robin
Hood / Alaska Tourism Council; John
Hyde / Southeast Alaska Tourism Council;
Marina Jarvis; Juneau Convention and
Visitors Bureau; Mark Kelley / Juneau
Convention and Visitors Bureau; Kristen
Kemmerling / Alaska Tourism Marketing
Council ;Muk Kumagai / Fairbanks
Convention and Visitors Bureau, MSCUA,
University Of Washington Libraries;
Nome Visitors Center; Paul Sanders /
Tourism North; Leslie Seam'n; Skagway
Convention and Visitors Bureau;
Southeast Alaska Tourism Council; Yutaka
Suzuki / Fairbanks Convention and
Visitors Bureau
Cover photograph:
Brian and Cherry Alexander

As every effort is made to provide accu-
rate information in this publication, we
would appreciate it if readers would call
our attention to any errors that may occur
by communicating with Apa Publications,
PO Box 7910, London SE1 1WE,
England. Fax: (44) 20 7403 0290;
e-mail: insight@apaguide.demon.co.uk

Distributed in the UK & Ireland by
GeoCenter International Ltd
The Viables Centre, Harrow Way
Basingstoke, Hampshire RG22 4BJ
Fax: (44 1256) 817-988

Distributed in the United States by
Langenscheidt Publishers, Inc.
46–35 54th Road, Maspeth, NY 11378
Tel: (718) 784-0055. Fax: (718) 784-0640

Worldwide distribution enquiries:
APA Publications GmbH & Co. Verlag KG
Singapore Branch, Singapore
38 Joo Koon Road, Singapore 628990
Tel: (65) 865-1600. Fax: (65) 861-6438

Printed in Singapore by
Insight Print Services (Pte) Ltd
38 Joo Koon Road, Singapore 628990
Tel: (65) 865-1600. Fax: (65) 861-6438

www.insightguides.com

THE LAST FRONTIER

They call it the Great Land, the Last Frontier – more than 580,000 sq. miles (1½ million sq. km) of land that taunted early explorers and still defies modern-day researchers, while exerting a fascination that attracts more and more travelers looking for something that a conventional vacation cannot give them. The hint of urban sophistication in Anchorage and Juneau rapidly gives way to the frontier, where outdoor survival skills are among the most useful attributes a resident can possess.

Alaska has lush rain-drenched forests and barren windswept tundras. There are lofty mountains, active volcanoes, and spectacular glaciers, three million lakes and endless swamps. Along with a handful of modern high-rise buildings there are countless one-room log cabins. Within hours of dining sumptuously in a first-class restaurant it is possible to tread on ground that has never known a human footprint: ground belonging to the grizzly and the wolf and shared only reluctantly with human beings.

This varied land is best viewed from a light plane or surveyed from a canoe; it cannot be seen properly from a car. Alaska is an outdoor world, a wilderness, a land of many faces, few of which can be explored by anyone simply moving from hotel to hotel.

The Alaskan adventure includes the sheer wonder of finding what hides beyond the horizon or over the next

Right: *warm welcome in Nome*

ridge. No one has ever seen it all and maybe no one ever will. That's the essence of Alaska. Something new, something different and something rare waits around the next bend in the river or twist in the trail.

Alaska is a land of remarkable diversity. It is the largest state in the USA, and the most sparsely populated. With approximately 621,400 residents, there is an average of about 1 sq. mile (2.5 sq. km) of land for each of them.

There's urban Alaska – mainly Anchorage, Fairbanks and Juneau. The latter is the capital, but it's a much smaller city than Anchorage. There's rural Alaska, which comprises the villages scattered throughout the land, mostly along major rivers or near the coast. And there's wilderness Alaska, vast regions of relatively untouched ground that knows only the whims of nature.

Communities have their attractions, and these are mostly

Above: *views to take your breath away*

friendly, easy-going communities, but it is the wilderness that beckons most travelers to Alaska. Where else in the world can you climb the highest peaks, follow an unexplored river bank, chill refreshments with ice broken from a glacier, or view hundreds of square miles of untrampled wildflowers, all with little more formality than a passport check when stepping from an airliner?

Almost all the cities and towns have companies which specialize in providing access to the wilderness. Charter air services, outdoor expedition ventures and a host of other related industries exist specifically to take travelers into remote regions – and to provide a way of earning a living in the wilderness, a factor which should not be overlooked, for it is a vital part of the state's economy.

Each Alaskan has his or her own favorite place, almost all of which are in the wilderness. In order to get the most out of their experience, visitors to Alaska should make the effort to spirit themselves away from civilization for a while and find a place of their own.

Ask anyone who has been to Alaska whether it was the thought of glaciers and mountains, or of a city, that lured them north. Very few will say the latter. People may be pleasantly surprised by Alaska's cities, but almost without exception they come to explore the great outdoors, the under-tamed wilderness that appeals so strongly to so many 21st-century urban dwellers.

Right: *a waterfall in the wilderness*

HISTORICAL HIGHLIGHTS

10,000 BC The Aleuts, the Eskimos (Inupiats and Yup'iks) and the Indians, which included the Athabascans and the coastal Tlingits and Haidas, settle in Alaska. Their way of life remains unchanged for many centuries.

1741 The first Russian ships arrive. Vitus Bering turns back and dies before he can reach home, but Alexei Chirikof lands on Prince William Island. The fur trade is established, and the Natives find themselves forced to hunt on the Russians' behalf.

1778 Captain James Cook visits the Aleutian Islands, prompting English interest in the fur trade.

1784 Grigor Ivanovich Shelikof arrives on Kodiak Island. He enslaves the Natives, then sets up the first permanent Russian settlement on Three Saints Bay, where he decides to introduce the Russian Orthodox religion.

1790 Alexander Baranof takes over the fur enterprise, treats the Natives more humanely than his predecessors, and moves the Russian colony to the present city of Kodiak.

1799 The Russian-American Company is formed.

1802 The Tlingits raze the Russian town of Mikhailovsk, near the site of present-day

Above: Captain James Cook

Sitka, on land they had sold to Baranof.

1812 Russia reaches a settlement with the United States over hunting rights.

1833 The British Hudson's Bay Company establishes a fur-trading outpost in Alaska and begins siphoning off trade.

Mid-19th century Russian power diminishes. British and Americans undermine the fur monopoly, and the Tlingits wage guerrilla war.

1866 A Western Union expedition produces the first scientific studies of Alaska.

1867 The US Congress buys Alaska from the Russians for $7.2 million.

1870s–80s Fish canneries are established around Nushagak Bay to exploit the huge runs of salmon. In the Aleutians fur seals and otters are slaughtered ruthlessly. Whalers pursue their quarries to the high Arctic.

1880 Gold is discovered at Silver Bow Basin, and the town of Juneau is founded.

Above: early settlers, Dexter Creek

1882 The Treadwell Mine, across the Gastineau Channel from Juneau, flourishes and the town of Douglas grows up.

1896 Gold is discovered in the Klondike, and the easiest route to it is by ship to Skagway. The White Pass and Chilkoot Trail to the gold fields are tackled by thousands of hopefuls.

1899 Gold is discovered at Nome in the far northwest.

1902 Gold is struck in Tanana Hills.

1903 The town of Fairbanks is founded on site of a trading post set up by entrepreneur E.T. Barnette.

Early 1900s Prospectors flock to Alaska from all over North America and Europe.

1910 Kennicott, the richest copper mine in the world, starts new operations in the Wrangell-St Elias mountains.

1942 Alaska Highway (Alcan) is constructed as a means of defense and an overland supply route to America's Russian allies, after sea routes are cut off following Japan's attack on Pearl Harbor. The Japanese land on Kiska and Attu islands. Villagers are interned in Japan for the rest of the war. Aleuts living in the Pribilofs and Aleutian Islands are evacuated.

1943 After a two-week battle, the Americans re-take Attu in May. In July, the Americans bomb Kiska, and the Japanese retreat on transport ships.

1957 Oil is discovered at the Swanson River on the Kenai Peninsula.

1959 Alaska becomes the 49th US state, a few months before Hawaii joins the Union.

Above: prospectors arrive by sea Right: an earthquake hits Anchorage

1964 The Good Friday earthquake hits South Central Alaska. Over 100 people are killed, mostly by tidal waves. Valdez, Seward, Cordova and Kodiak suffer the worst effects.

1968 A major oil find is made at Prudhoe Bay.

1971 Alaska Native Claims Settlement Act gives Natives title to 44 million acres (18 million hectares) of land, and $963 million, to be distributed among Native corporations.

1971–77 The construction of an ambitious trans-Alaska pipeline to Valdez creates thousands of jobs.

1976 The Alaska Permanent Fund is created to ensure long-term benefits from oil revenues.

1977 The trans-Alaska pipeline is completed. Oil begins to flow and the state economy booms, with most communities sharing some of the benefits.

1989 A tanker, *Exxon Valdez*, spills 11 million gallons (42 million liters) of oil into Prince William Sound. A huge clean-up operation is launched.

1990s to date The ecosystem of Prince William Sound recovers, although the long-term effects are not fully known. A decline in production at Prudhoe Bay leads to lay-offs and the realization that the oil boom will not last for ever. Low-impact ecotourism is encouraged.

PEOPLE AND CULTURE

Residents of the 49th State

Alaskans are a very special breed of people, accustomed to the cold and to the long hours of winter darkness, and resourceful enough to cope stoically with most things that climate and geography demand of them. And it's not just a case of putting up with hard conditions because they have no choice: some 25 percent of Alaska's population has moved there within the past five years. The average age in the state is only 32.

It is difficult to generalize about what constitutes a typical Alaskan: Alaska is so huge and the various parts of the state are so different from each other that the residents are bound to differ widely as well.

Anchorage (with 42 percent of the population), is a city of young professionals who seem to have little in common with people who live in the bush and call the Lower 48 states "America," as if they inhabited a separate country.

Above: Eskimo women

Native Alaskans

Anthropologists believe ancestors of the Alaska Natives migrated in three waves over a land bridge that joined Siberia and Alaska thousands of years ago. When Europeans first encountered Alaska Natives in the early 18th century, there were dozens of tribes and language groups throughout the region, from the Inupiat Eskimos in the Arctic region to the Tlingits in the Southeast. Today, these early Alaskans are divided into several main groups: the southeastern Coastal Indians (the Tlingits and Haidas), the Athabascans (also Indians), the Aleuts, and the two groups of Eskimos: Inupiat and Yup'ik.

Many Native Alaskans still live a subsistence lifestyle that depends on collecting meat and fish during summer months and preserving it for the long winter. In the south, Natives depend upon deer and salmon. In the Interior, the Athabascans fish in the rivers and hunt caribou and waterfowl. Further north, Eskimos hunt whale and seals. Most villages are in remote areas without roads to connect them with cities and luxuries such as large well-stocked grocery stores.

Although snow-machines are largely replacing dog sleds as a means of winter travel and boats with motors replace the skin boats that their ancestors used for fishing and hunting, Natives still follow traditional ways. But now they must have money to buy gasoline for their snow-machines and bullets for their guns. Their subsistence way of life requires modern tools and they meld the old with the new. It's a delicate balance. Natives struggle to keep their

Right: playing a seal-skin drum

own culture intact as they embrace the conveniences of modern society.

The 20th century brought numerous changes to Alaska's Native communities. Thirteen regional, four urban and 200 Native village corporations were formed to manage money and land received from the government as a result of the 1971 Alaska Native Claims Settlement Act. The measure approved the transfer of 44 million acres (18 million hectares) and $963 million to corporations in exchange for giving up their rights to the land.

The Russian Community

Some Alaskans came here long ago and stayed on, overcoming hardship and skepticism. Typical among them are the descendants of Russian immigrants in the Kenai Peninsula, Kodiak and Sitka. The first Russians came to Alaska in the late 18th century and established communities first in Kodiak, then in present-day Sitka, which became the headquarters of the fur trading Russian-American Company. Both towns retain strong Russian influences, but it is on the Kenai Peninsula that a strict Russian Orthodox community still survives, based around their "Island of Faith" near Anchor Point.

Survivors of persecution by the Orthodox Church, the government, and later the Stalinist purges, they call themselves "the

Above: *Russian Orthodox Church in Sitka*

Old Believers." Today they work in local businesses, or operate companies of their own, and manage their own fishing fleet. But their lives revolve around their religious beliefs. The study of holy books is mandatory during periods of fasting before Christmas and Lent. They wear traditional clothes: women and girls cover their heads with scarves, and men dress conservatively.

Bush Pilots

Among the most intrepid of Alaskans are the bush pilots – essential in a state where distances are so enormous. Alaska's first taste of aviation was courtesy of a local entrepreneur who flew an airplane over Fairbanks in honor of the 4th of July 1913. He loaded a disassembled airplane on a steamship, sailed it to Skagway, then transferred it to the White Pass and Yukon Railroad for the 125-mile (200-km) trip to Whitehorse, Yukon Territory.

Finally, he loaded his plane on a sternwheeler and steamed 800 miles (1,300 km) down the Yukon River, then 100 miles (160 km) up the Tanana and Chena rivers to Fairbanks. There he reassembled the plane, flew it for 11 minutes, then took it apart and carted it away.

The bush pilots' history really begins in the 1920s, when "Curtiss Jennies," surplus from World War I, were readily available for about $600. The first one

Right: *stern wheel on a steamer*

reached Alaska from New York in 1922. The old Jennies cruised at about 85 mph (135 kph) and carried only four hours' worth of fuel. The only non-stop, city-to-city trip possible was between Anchorage and Fairbanks. This meant the baggage compartment on longer flights was filled with fuel cans. Halfway between stops a pilot landed wherever he could, poured in fuel, and took off again.

From this beginning came the Alaska-based air carriers operating today. Slowly but surely the planes have evolved, making it possible for passengers to fly in first-class comfort and luxury. The plane is warm, it flies above most of the weather, and sophisticated electronics guide it almost effortlessly to its destination. It's a far cry from the days of the Alaskan bush pilot, but even if conditions are easier, the pilots still have to turn out in all weathers and people still rely on them to turn up in emergencies, and to deliver the mail.

The Life of a Trapper

Life in the Alaskan bush can be exhilarating, but it is very hard and often tedious. Trapping is one of the least profitable professions there is, and one that has changed little over the years, but there are those who love the life. One change, which has made life easier, is that many trappers now use snow-machines instead of traditional dog sleds. This has its disadvantages, of course: after all, dogs don't break down, as machines do,

Left: seaplanes help deliver the mail

and a trapper now always needs to carry survival gear and show-shoes for walking home when the engine inexplicably dies.

Some trappers have chosen to stick to the dog sleds – a hard but rewarding way of life. These trappers must be able to control a sled drawn by a dozen huskies, capable of doing some 60 miles (100 km) a day on a good trail, in temperatures dipping to as low as –50°F (–45°C).

Whether using a snow-machine or a dog sled, a trapper must remain constantly alert for unseen dangers: thin ice, deadly water hidden under deep snow, irritable moose, open creeks, or a fresh tree blown down across the trail – these are all hazards that crop up suddenly and without warning.

The trappers' yearly cycle involves putting up food in summer and fall, and trapping and woodcutting in winter and spring. The weekly cycle is measured by the mail plane and the trapline rounds; and the daily cycle is one of mushing dogs, maintaining equipment and feeding fires.

Above: *controlling a dog sled is difficult work*

The Alcan

In 1942, while the world was at war, thousands of American soldiers spent eight months building a 1,500-mile (2,400-km) highway from Dawson Creek, British Columbia, to Delta Junction, Alaska, just south of Fairbanks.

Construction of the Alaska–Canada Military Highway (the Alcan) was approved by President Franklin D. Roosevelt after the bombing of Pearl Harbor in 1941. Its purpose was to form an overland supply route to America's Russian allies on the other side of the Bering Strait. The road linked the contiguous United States to Alaska.

Today, the former military road provides a leisurely and scenic way for visitors to reach Alaska year-round. The Alcan more or less follows its original path, wiggling its way northwest through British Columbia and the Yukon into Alaska's Interior. But what was once a wilderness adventure road is now a mostly paved highway. The scenery is still breathtaking and the chances of seeing wildlife are good, and continual road improvements have eased many of the dangers that once made driving to Alaska an ordeal.

It is not a Sunday drive, however. It's only two lanes wide, often without a center line, and although the entire length is asphalt surfaced, sections have to be repaved continually. Drivers have to watch for wildlife and construction workers on the road as well as chuckholes, gravel breaks and deteriorating shoulders. On the northern portion of the highway, frost heaves – the result of the freezing and thawing of the ground – cause the pavement to ripple.

Above: international signpost, near Dawson City

But despite the rigors of the road, the trip is made by more than 100,000 people every year. You'll often see cars sporting bumper stickers that proclaim "I survived the Alcan Highway."

The Pipeline

In 1968, oil was discovered at Prudhoe Bay on the Arctic Coast. Drilling at such a remote location would be difficult enough – but transporting the resulting crude to refineries in the Lower 48 states seemed almost impossible. The solution was to build a pipeline to carry the oil across Alaska to the southern port of Valdez where it would be loaded onto tanker ships.

Between the two points were three mountain ranges, active fault lines, miles and miles of unstable *muskeg* (boggy ground underlain with permafrost) and the migration paths of caribou and moose. To counteract the unstable ground and allow animal crossings, half the 800-mile (1,280-km) pipeline is elevated on supports that hold the pipe and its cargo of hot oil high enough

Above: *the trans-Alaska pipeline*

to keep it from melting the permafrost and destroying the terrain. To help the pipeline survive an earthquake, it was laid out in a zigzag pattern, so that it would roll with the earth instead of breaking up. The first oil arrived at Valdez on July 28, 1977. The total cost of the pipeline and related projects, including the tanker terminal at Valdez, 12 pumping stations and the Yukon River Bridge, was $8 billion.

The Earthquake

On March 27, 1964, the Good Friday earthquake struck South-central Alaska, churning the earth for four minutes. An estimated 8.7 on the Richter scale, the quake is one of the most powerful ever recorded, killing 103 people. Most of them were drowned by the tidal waves *(tsunamis)* that tore apart the towns of Valdez and Chenega. Throughout the Prince William Sound region towns and ports were destroyed, land uplifted or shoved downward, islands tilted. Ports at Valdez and Cordova were beyond repair.

Above: glacier in Prince William Sound

At Valdez, an Alaska Steamship Company ship was lifted by a huge wave over the docks and out to sea. Amazingly, most hands survived, although most of those who were waiting on the dockside to greet the ship were swept to their deaths.

In Anchorage, huge chunks of road asphalt piled on top of each other like shingles. At Seldovia, near the junction of Kachemak Bay and Cook Inlet, fish processing facilities and an active fishing fleet were laid waste. On Kodiak, a tidal wave wiped out the villages of Afognak, Old Harbor and Kaguyak. Seward, a thriving port town at the southern terminus of the Alaska Central Railroad, also lost its harbor.

Despite the extent of the catastrophe, many devastated communities were swiftly rebuilt. Valdez now stands a few miles from the ruins of its former self.

The Klondike Gold Rush

Gold was first discovered in the Yukon in 1896. During the next two years 100,000 people poured into Dawson in the Klondike in search of gold. Although Dawson is in Canada, the best way to reach it was by ship from Seattle to Skagway, 600 miles (960 km) across one of two treacherous passes – the White Pass from Skagway or the Chilkoot from Dyea. The former was believed to be slightly easier, but it was controlled by "Soapy" Smith – a villain who virtually ran Skagway during the gold boom – and stories of men being robbed and murdered were

Right: a contemporary gold panner

rife. On the Chilkoot Pass it was the elements that were the killers. The journey was made more difficult by the fact that, after some of the early prospectors died of starvation, the Canadian government insisted that each man should take a year's supplies – which weighed roughly a ton.

Prospectors crossing the Chilkoot and White passes to Dawson during the coldest winter in living memory set up encampments en route. Once the winter and the hazards of the trail were over,

they had to face the rapids and whirlpools of lakes and rivers which they tackled in hand-made boats – denuding forests to build them. On Palm Sunday, 1898, sunshine melted the snow and an avalanche engulfed a Chilkoot Trail camp, killing 70.

Dreams of gold kept them going, but by the time most of them reached Dawson, the productive claims were already allocated. The early prospectors had struck lucky with the claims closer to the surface, but by the time the great influx of hopefuls arrived they were digging for gold some 50 ft (15 meters) beneath the surface. To reach it they had to force their way through permafrost, burning it to soften the land, then sinking shafts which might, or might not, hit the right spot.

While some people became rich, and others found enough to give them security, many of the stampeders, having sunk everything they owned in the enterprise, were ruined.

Above: *the White Pass Railroad*

Native Crafts

Craft items created by Alaskan Natives originally had either a practical or a cultural use. Carvers created masks for ceremonies, totem poles to tell the histories of clans, and Chilkat blankets for special dancing, or to be presented as tokens of esteem. These days, although much Native art still serves traditional purposes, many objects are made for sale. Dance fans and masks, for example, are still used in ceremonies today, but they are also sold as souvenirs – often such sales are a welcome source of income for villagers.

Natives from different parts of Alaska excel in different types of art. Doll-making has been an Eskimo art form for 2,000 years. The detailed dolls with carved faces and fur parkas portray Eskimo ways of life, from hunters to berry-pickers and skin sewers. The Athabascans are known for their colorful beadwork, usually flowers on tanned moose hide, and incorporating por-cupine quills and buttons. The Aleuts are masters at making tightly woven grass baskets, often decorated with multicolored embroidery.

Visitors wanting to buy should look out for the authenticity symbol – a silver hand with the designation "Native Handicraft."

Totem Poles

Totem poles, some as high as 60 ft (18 meters) tall, are still made by Native woodworkers in the Northwest of the

Right: *furry fashion*

state. Figures, or totems, on the poles are used to tell a story, legend or event. The totemic symbols are usually animals, such as bears, eagles or killer whales. Their significance lies in myth – stories passed down through generations about how certain animals may have affected the destiny of ancestors.

Poles would be found clustered along a village's shore in front of clan houses, or on the fronts of private houses, and often in cemeteries. According to some early accounts of Tlingit life, deceased clan members were cremated and their ashes placed in these poles.

Missionaries and other outsiders contributed to the destruction and neglect of many totem poles. Since the 1930s, many have been restored, some of which now stand in totem parks near villages like Klawock and Saxman and at the Totem Heritage Center in Ketchikan.

The Northern Lights

The northern lights, or *aurora borealis*, are nature's own special event. They are seen more often and more vividly in and around Fairbanks in Alaska's Interior. In winter this extraordinary show can last for hours; in mid-summer the sky is too light for it to be visible. But if it is late August or September when you visit, you will be able to see the wonderful dancing lights illuminate the sky night after night.

Above: pole in a totem park, Ketchikan

The Midnight Sun

The best place to see the midnight sun is in the far north of Alaska, at the northernmost tip of the American continent, where the sun does not set from mid-May to early August. It's pretty impressive elsewhere, too. In Fairbanks (easier to reach than the far north) a great Midnight Sun festival is held on the weekend closest to the solstice, June 21 *(see page 71)*.

Flora

Alaska's fauna is well known – and it is mentioned numerous times in the A–Z section of this book, but Alaska is also a state surprisingly rich in flora. The growing season is short, but critical, since flowering plants provide nutrients for the many animals that feed on them, and a bad year for flora is a bad one for dependent fauna, too. Plants of the same species may bloom as much as six weeks apart, depending on their location.

Above: the Northern Lights

In mid-summer, whole fields and hillsides of bushy, bright pink fireweed saturate many parts of Alaska. Fireweed blooms from the bottom of the stem to the top, and Alaskans say that when the top flower finally blooms, it means that summer is almost over. It isn't at all unusual for dwarf fireweed, also known as river beauty, to cover completely gravel bars along glacial streams. Probably the most commonly seen plant in Alaska, it gets its name not from its color but from its ability to renew itself rapidly after a fire, as its deep roots manage to escape the conflagration.

Above the treeline lies the tundra, a lumpy carpet of bushes, grasses and flowers. Soil is scarce here and flowers cling to the edges of rocky slopes or windswept meadows. Many have developed unusual adaptations that allow them to survive wind and often brutal temperatures.

Above: *a walker and his dog*

Bearberries, which grow close to the ground in rocky alpine areas and on the tundra, arctic poppies, whose inner temperature may be 18°F (10°C) warmer than the air outside and low-bush cranberries, whose berries stay on the bush through the winter, are among Alaska's most resilient plants.

Food

Alaska is not a place for gourmet meals, but all its cities offer a variety of good places to eat. Fast-food chains can be found in larger communities, as can ethnic restaurants serving Thai, Vietnamese and Mexican food. Once you get outside the major towns, however, food ranges from great home cooking to rather bland and uninteresting fare. One thing that is consistent wherever you go, however, is that prices are high. The rationale behind this is that virtually all food products must be flown in and that staff costs are also high.

As you would expect in a state where the waters are so bountiful and fishing is such an important part of the economy, many Alaskan restaurants serve outstanding fish and seafood dishes. Both Alaska King crab and Dungeness crab are often on the menu when in season. Other shellfish, such as local shrimp, scallops, mussels and oysters, are also often available, as are fresh salmon and halibut.

Above: Alaska King crab

A–Z OF ALASKA

Admiralty Island

Angoon is the only settlement in Admiralty Island National Monument, a largely wilderness preserve which can be reached by air or sea from Sitka or Juneau, and which is famous for its salmon and, especially, the large numbers of brown bears – some reckon there are as many as 1,700 on the island.

Anchorage

This port city didn't get a good purchase on life until 1915, but in the decades since it has developed from a railroad tent camp to a city of high-rise offices and ethnic restaurants. Anchorage is not the state capital but it is home to 42 percent of the state's residents with a population of a quarter of a million. It is the largest metropolis in Alaska. Laid out on a grid system, it's very easy to find your way around. *www.ci.anchorage.ak.us*

ALASKA CENTER FOR THE PERFORMING ARTS

This building is viewed by some as a monstrosity and by others as architecturally innovative, richly adding to the beauty of the downtown area. Much of the interior, including carpets and upholstery, has been designed by Alaskan artists, and it is decorated with numerous Native masks. Tours are organized three days a week in summer.

Performances by the Anchorage Symphony Orchestra and the Anchorage Concert Association begin in the fall. The Concert Association presents world-class performers in music and dance. *www.alaskapac.org*

Left: *Portage Lake and Glacier, near Anchorage*

ANCHORAGE COASTAL WILDLIFE REFUGE

On the southern edge of town and locally known as Potter Marsh, this 2,300-acre (920-hectare) wetland area is the nesting ground for migratory birds during the summer. Bald eagles, Arctic terns, trumpeter swans and many species of ducks are common. Canada geese and mallards raise their young here. From the boardwalk above the channel, huge red salmon are visible from mid-July to September as they return to spawn in nearby Rabbit Creek.

ALASKA HERITAGE LIBRARY AND MUSEUM

Situated in the lobby of the National Bank of Alaska, the museum has a large selection of Native art and artifacts and a number of works by Sydney Laurence (1865–1940), known as "the painter of the north." *www.nationalbankofalaska.com/heritage.htm*

ALASKA NATIVE ARTS & CRAFTS ASSOCIATION

A non-profit organization in the Post Office Mall, the Association's works include carved walrus ivory, soapstone and horn, and intricate baskets. Authentic Native-made handicrafts are identified by a tag showing a silver hand or stating "Authentic Native Handicraft."

ALASKA PUBLIC LANDS INFORMATION CENTER

If you are planning on visiting national parks or taking part in any outdoor activities you will find this place invaluable. You can see wildlife exhibits, watch videos on the various regions and activities available, and generally pick up all the information you'll need. *www.nps.gov/aplic*

ANCHORAGE MUSEUM OF HISTORY AND ART

Among the museum's permanent collections are the Alaska Gallery, with historical exhibits, and an excellent selection of Native art and works by travelers, explorers and early residents, beautifully displayed in skylit galleries. The museum shop sells books, prints and Native crafts.

BIKE TRAILS

Anchorage is a great place for cyclists, with more than 120 miles (190 km) of paved paths, and plenty of bikes for hire. The best known and most scenic route is the **Tony Knowles Coastal Trail**, which starts near Elderberry Park on 2nd Avenue. The trail is 12 miles (20 km) long and parallels Knik Arm, continuing past Westchester Lagoon, and ending at Kincaid Park. In winter, the path becomes a cross-country ski trail. There are a number of other bike routes in town.

Left: Native art in Anchorage Museum Above: cyclists on the trail

EARTHQUAKE PARK
Founded on the spot where, during the 1964 earthquake, some 130 acres (52 hectares) of land fell into the inlet, and 75 houses were destroyed. A walking trail and new, museum-quality interpretive signs make it well worth the stop.

IMAGINARIUM
While primarily aimed at children, this award-winning science museum has a wealth of exhibits and hands-on experiences that are also popular with adults. If you want to know more about marine life, wetlands and the solar system, this is a good place to find out. *www.imaginarium.com*

OOMINGMAK MUSK OX PRODUCERS' CO-OP
The co-op sells garments of musk ox wool, called *qiviut (kee-vee-ute)* that are made in Eskimo villages. It is believed that the soft lightweight wool is the warmest material in the world.

OSCAR ANDERSON HOUSE MUSEUM
Set in attractive Elderberry Park. this is Anchorage's first wood-frame house, built by Swedish immigrant Anderson in 1915.

SACKS CAFÉ
An intimate atmosphere and very good seafood are on offer at Sacks Café. Don't miss trying the Alaskan specialties like baked halibut, salmon or steamed crab. *www.sackscafe.com*

Above:** killer whales...* ***Right: *...and their bones at Barrow*

Barrow

At the northernmost tip of North America, Barrow is Alaska's
largest Eskimo community. The midnight sun here does not set
from mid-May to early August, and visitors have the chance to
stand on the continent's northern edge, a windswept stretch of
beach, often shrouded in fog, and usually littered with ice.

For winter visitors, the northern lights are another attraction,
but they are equally apparent in Fairbanks *(see page 34)*, which
is a great deal more accessible than Barrow.

Most people come here as part of a package tour: travel
agencies offer trips to Barrow from Anchorage and Fairbanks.
And most stop at Pepe's North of the Border Restaurant,
Barrow's most famous eating house.

Cape Krusenstern

Cape Krusenstern stretches into polar waters in northwestern
Alaska. Hidden beneath beach ridges are archeological treasures
reaching back 4,000 years. This chronicle of early man brought
about the establishment of the 560,000-acre (226,600-hectare)

Cape Krusenstern National Monument in 1980. Charter planes and boats headquartered in Kotzebue (which has a jet service from both Anchorage and Fairbanks.) take infrequent visitors to the monument, 10 miles (16 km) northwest across Kotzebue Sound. Planes can land on some beaches, and floatplanes put down on nearby lagoons. Travelers are free to explore archeological zones, but no digging for artifacts or causing other disturbance is allowed.

Cape Krusenstern lacks visitor services – no public shelters or campgrounds – and receives only about 3,500 visitors a year. This is a bring-your-own-shelter place, and that goes for stove, food and water, so come prepared to be self-sustaining.

At the southern tip of the monument, Sheshalik, "Place of White Whales," is a traditional gathering place for hunters of beluga, the small, white, toothed whale.

A great variety of waterfowl can be seen in summer. The fall brings walrus, Arctic foxes, wolves, wolverines, red foxes, lynx, mink, short-tailed weasels, tundra hare, and – rarely nowadays – bear. *www.nps.gov/cakr*

Denali National Park

Denali is one of the world's greatest wildlife sanctuaries, billed as the ultimate Alaskan experience. The park entrance is situated on George Parks Highway, 240 miles (385 km) north of Anchorage and 120 miles (190 km) south of Fairbanks. Access

Above: *a moose stops for a drink*

is also provided by the Alaska Railroad, which has a daily service from both Anchorage and Fairbanks.

Denali National Park Hotel offers an array of services, including private wildlife bus tours, river rafting and flightseeing excursions. Complete packages are available, including transportation to the park.

Shuttle buses from the Visitor Center make all-day trips around the park, stopping whenever animals are seen. Moose are the biggest animals in the park;

grizzly bears, caribou, and Dall sheep are also frequently seen and, less frequently, wolves.

Sable Pass, at 3,900 ft (1,190 meters), is a tundra region, located above the treeline, and it is grizzly bear country. It's one of the best places in the world for viewing the most dangerous animal in North America.

The brightly colored cliffs of **Polychrome Pass** are volcanic rocks formed 50 million years ago. This is a good place to watch for wolves. A local pack uses these flats as its hunting grounds, especially in spring when caribou are in migration.

Caribou, the most social of the large Denali animals, are commonly seen in the **Highway Pass** area, especially in the spring. *www.nps.gov.dena*

Right: *camping on top of the world*

Fairbanks

To reach Fairbanks, it's either a long drive up the Alaska and Richardson Highways or a flight to Fairbanks International Airport. In winter, the town has 3 hours 40 minutes of sunlight, and ice fog hangs in the still air. But in summer daylight lasts for 22 hours. There's an attractive park, Golden Heart Plaza, and lots of shopping: gold-nugget jewelry, Native handicrafts from the Interior, and furs.

Fairbanks hosts numerous events, including the Alaska State Fair, the Winter Carnival, the North American Open Sled Dog Championship, and the Yukon–Quest sled dog race, and it is the best place to see the Northern Lights *(see page 22)*. Fairbanks residents do not allow the summer solstice to slip by uncelebrated: The Fairbanks Gold Panners baseball team plays the Midnight Sun game at Growden Field with the first pitch crossing the plate at 10.45pm – under natural light. *www.explorefairbanks.com*

ALASKALAND

Alaskaland is a 44-acre (18-hectare) city park with numerous attractions, including the Mining Valley containing gold-extracting machinery and sluice boxes; the Mining Town with an assortment of original structures from the boom-town period;

Above: train at El Dorado mine, Fairbanks

the Gold Rush Town, which is packed with craft shops; and the *Sternwheeler Nenana*, a classic paddlewheeler, listed in the National Register of Historic Places.

GOLD DREDGE NO. 8

The easiest of the gold dredges to visit is at Mile 9 (15 km) Old Steese Highway. The five-deck ship is over 250 ft (76 meters) long and displaced 1,065 tons as it plied the gold pay dirt of Goldstream and Engineer creeks. Tours of the dredge (including gold panning – you keep what you pan) are available daily during summer.

NORTHWARD BUILDING

More commonly known as the Ice Palace, this was the first steel-girded skyscraper in the Interior, and became the inspiration for Edna Ferber's 1958 novel, *Ice Palace*.

ST MATTHEW'S EPISCOPAL CHURCH

The stained-glass windows of St Matthew's are of special interest as they portray images of Jesus, Mary and Joseph with the dark hair and features of Alaskan Natives.

UNIVERSITY OF ALASKA MUSEUM

The museum is one of the best in the state, dividing Alaska's regions with an interdisciplinary approach to each which includes cultural artifacts and scientific equipment. Displays include prehistoric

Right: panning for gold

objects extricated from the permanently frozen ground: one is a 36,000-year-old bison carcass. The Native Cultures displays offer an introduction to the Athabascan, Eskimo, Aleut and Tlingit cultures. There are also tours at the **Geophysical Institute**, a world center for arctic and aurora research, during which a spectacular film of the *aurora borealis* is shown. A free off-campus tour is offered to the **Large Animal Research Facility**, formerly known as the Musk Ox Farm. *www.uaf.edu/museum*

Gates of the Arctic National Park

A preserved wilderness of 8 million acres (3.2 million hectares) in the central Brooks Range in the heart of northern Alaska, Gates is 200 miles (320 km) northwest of Fairbanks, and the same distance south of Barrow *(see page 31)*. No maintained roads exist within the park – no phones, TVs, radios, gas stations, restaurants, stores or hotels. No emergency services are available: no hospitals, police or fire stations. There is one permanent ranger station at **Anaktuvuk Pass**, a Native village in the middle of the park.

Above: *at home on the range*

Bettles is the gateway to Gates. You can take a scheduled flight from Fairbanks to this friendly little outpost, then hire an air taxi. Or, if you have the stamina, drive up **Dalton Highway** through wild wilderness to **Coldfoot**. At the Coldfoot Services Truckstop motel rooms are available. A summer visitor center is operated here.

The most popular trip is to the north fork of the Koyukuk River, where the peaks, Frigid Craigs and Boreal Mountain, stand guard. They are the climax of a 10-day backpacking trip that starts at Summit Lake and ends at Chimney Lake.

Float trips can be arranged throughout the park. Winter cross-country ski trips, dog sled rides and ice fishing are available at beautiful, fish-filled **Walker Lake**, where a few private cabins are the only places to sleep indoors in the park. *www.nps.gov/gaar*

Glacier Bay National Park

Located at the northern end of Alaska's southeastern Panhandle, Glacier Bay encompasses 3.3 million acres (1.3 million hectares). Most visitors arrive here on large cruise-ships or package tours, but you can reach Gustavus by air and boat charters from Juneau.

In a land comprising three climatic zones – marine to arctic – seven different ecosystems support a wide variety of plant and animal life. Near Gustavus, an ecosystem of sandy grassland, coniferous forests and damp marshes provides habitat for cranes, otters, wolves, bears, coyotes and moose.

Above: *the icy waters of Glacier Bay*

Endangered humpback whales feed in the waters of Glacier Bay in the summer, and killer and minke whales are sometimes seen. Sea lions and otters, harbor seals and porpoises are also frequently sighted.

Bartlett Cove lies within a region dominated by coastal western hemlock and Sitka spruce, where bald eagles fly overhead. *www.nps.gov/glba*

Juneau

Alaska's capital is a small town in terms of population, but its 3,108 sq. miles (8,050 sq. km) make it the biggest town in North America and second biggest in the world – exceeded only by Kiruna in Sweden. It's a lively place with busy docks and meandering, narrow streets and alleys. South Franklin Street is lined with art galleries and shops that feature Alaskan ivory, jade, totemic wood carvings and leatherwork. There is also the Alaskan Hotel Bar, which retains its gold rush-era decor. *www.traveljuneau.com*

ALASKA STATE MUSEUM

Inuit culture is represented here in the form of intricate ivory carvings and a 40-ft (12-meter) *umiak*, or skin boat, of the type used for whale- and walrus-hunting along the ice floes of the Arctic Ocean. Southeast Alaska's ancient way of life is reflected in a re-created community house, complete with priceless totemic

Above: a view of downtown Juneau

carvings, and the Athabascan Natives, from the Interior, are represented by a birch bark canoe, weapons and bead-decorated moosehide garments.

Most notable is the "eagle tree," just inside the front entrance: a towering spruce that rises from ground level to the ceiling of the second floor. In a fork of the branches a nest holds an authentic-looking young bald eagle, with wings outstretched.

HIKING TRAILS

Juneau has a rich variety of hiking trails, easily reached from the dockside and city center. All the starting points are clearly marked and there is information available about routes. Among the best-known trails are Mt Roberts, Perseverance, and Mt Juneau.

MARINE PARK

Overlooking the city's dock and wharf area, this is a small, pleasurable place of benches and shady trees situated near the ramp where cruise-ship passengers land after being lightered from ships at anchor offshore. This is where half of Juneau eats its lunch on sunny summer days. Street vendors offer food that ranges from halibut to hot dogs, and from tacos to Vietnamese spring rolls.

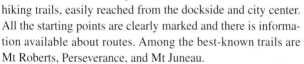

Right: companions on a hiking trail

ST NICHOLAS RUSSIAN ORTHODOX CHURCH
This tiny, onion-domed, octagon-shaped church was built in 1894 at the specific request of the principal chief of the Tlingits of Juneau. It is the oldest original Orthodox church in Southeast Alaska.

STATE CAPITOL BUILDING
Built in the 1930s, the capitol's halls and offices have recently been refurbished to reflect that era. Tours daily in summer.

STATE OFFICE BUILDING
Visitors can stroll through the sky-lighted great hall and, on Friday at noon, listen to a giant old Kimball theater organ, a magnificent relic of Juneau's silent movie days.

Katmai National Park
The scenery in this isolated location is breathtaking, the weather is unstable and the winds can be life-threatening. Located 290

Above: *a humpback breaks the surface*

air miles (465 km) from Anchorage, the park is a haven for lovers of the unspoiled wilderness. Katmai can be reached by an hour's flight from Anchorage to King Salmon, and a 20-minute trip by floatplane or amphibian chartered from King Salmon to Brooks Camp.

In the immediate vicinity of Brooks Camp on Naknek Lake bears can be seen in July and September from a safe viewing platform as they feed on spawning salmon. A tour bus provides transportation to the scene of volcanic devastation in the Valley of Ten Thousand Smokes. Nearly a century after the eruption, the valley is still awe-inspiring. Ash, pumice and rocks produced over 40 sq. miles (100 sq. km) of lunar landscape, sculpted by wind and water.

A series of small lakes and rivers provide opportunities for canoeing, kayaking and fishing. Rainbow trout, lake trout, char, pike and grayling are popular sport fish here, as well as sockeye, coho, king, pink and chum salmon. Nearly 1 million salmon return each year to the Naknek River.

Although brown bears are the main attraction there is a great deal of other wildlife: moose, caribou, land otter, wolverine, marten, weasel, mink, lynx, fox, wolf, muskrat, beaver and hare all inhabit the park. Off coastal waters, seals, sea lions, sea otters and beluga and gray whales can be seen. *www.nps.gov/katm*

Above: *brown bears in Katmai Park*

Kenai Peninsula

The entire peninsula, which covers 9,050 sq. miles (23,000 sq. km), is within easy driving distance of Anchorage. It is bordered by Prince William Sound and the Gulf of Alaska on the east and Cook Inlet on the west, and attached to the mainland of Southcentral Alaska by a narrow mountainous neck of land at the north. The peninsula was originally home to Dena'ina Indians, a branch of the Athabascan family, and to Eskimos. Their descendants still live here, mostly in small, remote villages, but now account for something less than 10 percent of the population. *www.kenaipeninsula.org*

HOPE

A mining community of about 200, founded in the late 1890s, Hope is the site of the oldest schoolhouse in Alaska, and the Hope and Sunrise Mining Museum. It is also an ideal site for pink salmon fishing, moose, caribou and black bear hunting, and it

Above: *taking a view at Kenai Peninsula*

is the head of the Resurrection Trail, one of the most popular hiking areas on the peninsula.

HOMER

Sitting on the shore of Kachemak Bay, Homer is a pleasant little town in a picturesque setting between mountains and sea, and best known for the Homer Spit, which extends 5 miles (8 km) out into the bay. Major attractions are  boat tours and halibut-fishing trips. There's also the Pratt Museum, which focuses on marine life in the bay. It has an excellent exhibit on the effects of the *Exxon Valdez* oil spill.

Homer has quite a reputation as a local arts center, and there are a number of art galleries, some displaying pottery and jewelry as well as paintings. In downtown Homer there are several good restaurants and souvenir shops. *www.homeralaska.org*

KENAI

The largest city on the peninsula and the oldest permanent settlement, founded by Russian fur traders and Orthodox priests in the late 18th century, Kenai has the peninsula's most regular scheduled flights. It is also the home port to a good share of the peninsula's drift-net fishing fleet. During spring, the flats along the river mouth are temporary nesting ground for thousands of snow geese, and in the summer a parade of boats can be seen in their quest for red salmon.

Above: *visiting Homer*

Kenai Visitors' and Cultural Center features exhibits and displays of the town's Native and Russian history, and on the industries that currently fuel the area: oil and commercial fishing. On Mission Street, the Holy Assumption Russian Orthodox Church is the oldest Orthodox place of worship in Alaska. Follow Mission Street to Riverview Avenue to the Beluga Whale Lookout where, in early summer, you can watch white whales feeding on salmon in the river. *www.visitkenai.com*

KENAI FJORDS NATIONAL PARK

Declared a national monument in 1978 and designated a national park two years later, the park is home to porpoises, sea otters, sea lions, humpback and orca whales, puffins and bald eagles as well as the rugged coastal fjords for which it is named, and the glaciers which, for many, are its chief attraction. Several local tour operators offer frequent wildlife cruises into the park, starting from Seward's Small Boat Harbor.

Most of the park is only accessible by boat: the only vehicle access is to the northwest of Seward, at Exit Glacier Road. Exit Glacier is the most easily accessible point of the Harding Icefield, a remnant of the Ice Age that caps a section of the Kenai Mountains 50 miles (80 km) long and 30 miles (50 km) wide.

Above: *sunset over the Kenai mountains* **Right:** *Kenai Lake*

KENAI LAKE

The lake holds Dolly Varden, lake trout, rainbow trout and white-fish, king, silver and red salmon. Trophy rainbow trout, some weighing as much as 20 lbs (9 kg), are caught here by spin- and fly-fishing enthusiasts, and catch-and-release fishing is widely practiced. Rafting is another popular activity, and several local businesses offer fishing and float trips.

Just outside of the Cooper Landing area at the confluence of the Kenai and Russian rivers, is the turnoff to the Russian River Campground. The 20-mile (32-km) Russian Lakes Trail is a delightful and not over-demanding hike, with cabins en route.

KENAI NATIONAL WILDLIFE REFUGE

Established to preserve the moose population, the refuge is also the habitat of coyotes, grizzlies, caribou, and wolves. It comprises the western slopes of the Kenai Mountains, and spruce and birch forested lowlands bordering Cook Inlet. Among the major recreational areas is the 20-mile (32-km) Skilak Lake Loop, which intersects the Sterling Highway near the Visitor Center. This road

goes to Skilak Lake, and provides access to several other smaller lakes, streams and some 200 miles (320 km) of trails in the area. The most arduous trail is the Skilak Lookout Trail, which takes you up some 1,450 ft (440 meters) and provides stunning views.

SEWARD

Seward is the northern terminus for most cruise-ships crossing the Gulf of Alaska. An attractive city of about 3,000 residents, Seward was founded in 1903, and was for years Alaska's leading port city. It was eventually eclipsed by Anchorage, and the 1964 earthquake devastated the economy. Twenty years later, it began to regain its financial legs and now is once again a thriving port. The Seward Historical Museum features a film on the effects of the 1964 earthquake.

One of the area's main attractions is Resurrection Bay. Charter boats are available at the city harbor, as are kayak rentals. The state ferry system also has a dock in Seward, offering trips to Kodiak and the Prince William Sound areas.

Seward's newest and biggest attraction is the Alaska SeaLife Center built on a 7-acre (3-hectare) site next to the Marine Edu-

cation Center on the shores of Resurrection Bay. This marine science enterprise combines research on saving marine species and aiding recovery from industrial damage, with the rehabilitation of maimed or stranded birds and mammals. It also aims to provide education and entertainment for its thousands of visitors.

Seward has an exuberant 4th of July celebration, and also the annual Silver Salmon Derby, a week-long fishing contest that offers the highest prize money in Alaska. It begins on the second Saturday of August.

Kodiak Island

A shift of the wind can change Kodiak Island from a desolate, windswept, rain-pounded rock isolated from the rest of the world by fog, to a shimmering emerald of grass, spruce trees and snow-capped mountains glowing an extra-ordinary pink in the sunrise.

Except for several Native villages, the populated portion of Kodiak Island is confined to the road system – less than 100 miles (160 km) of it. Some parts are only fit for 4-wheel-drive vehicles, but others can be driven in an ordinary car. The six coastal villages on the island are accessible only by plane or boat; if you want to visit one of them, you need to make arrangements in advance.

In summer salmon can be seen jumping in the bays and swimming up the rivers. July and August are the best months for salmon-watching or fishing. Occasionally sea lions come into the bays.

Left: *cruise ship in the gulf* **Right:** *sailing near Seward*

It is very tempting to stop at every twist of the road, and there are no restrictions on exploring the beaches, walking in the forests, climbing the mountains, or simply enjoying the wildflowers.

In spring and falls whales pass the Fossil Beach end of the island migrating to and from their northern summer feeding grounds. *www.kodiak.org*

BAROMETER MOUNTAIN

At the end of Kodiak Island airport runway Barometer Mountain (2,450 ft/745 meters) is so called because the peak is only visible in good weather.

KODIAK

A town of 6,800 people perched precariously on a small ledge of land between ocean swells and mountains, Kodiak is home to a multi-million-dollar fishing fleet which ranges from the Pacific Northwest to Norton Sound. It's a town with a rich history: artifacts of the indigenous Koniag culture surface near remnants of the 18th–19th-century Russian period or World War II bunkers, derelict whaling stations, or collapsing herring-rendering plants. Just under the topsoil is a layer of volcanic ash that covered the town in 1912 and still drifts about, leaving a coating of fine, white dust. White spruce tree skeletons guard the salt marshes, monuments to the land subsidence that occurred during the 1964 earthquake and tidal wave.

Above: *Alutiiq dancer in Kodiak* ***Right:*** *Orthodox domes*

The best window on Koniag culture – much of which was absorbed by the Russian one – is at the Alutiiq Museum. This Native-owned research museum interprets artifacts from Koniag-directed archeological digs. Visitors can also join digs on six-day sessions at remote sites in the Dig Afognak program.

The small Baranof Museum contains displays of Koniag artifacts and clothing as well as items from the Russian and early American periods. It is housed in Erskine House, which has been designated a National Historic Landmark, and is the oldest Russian building in North America.

The Holy Resurrection Russian Orthodox Church's two blue onion domes are the town's most outstanding landmarks. Treasures of the church include many brilliantly colored icons. Orthodoxy still plays a significant role in the Kodiak community.

KODIAK NATIONAL WILDLIFE REFUGE

The refuge can only be reached by air or sea. This mountainous wilderness, covering two-thirds of the island, belongs to bears and foxes, rabbits and birds, muskrats and otters. Most people

come here to see the brown bears – the world's largest carnivores. The best and safest way is to take one of the (expensive) charter plane tours on offer in Kodiak. Alternatively, several wilderness lodges on the island have bear-viewing packages; and a wildlife refuge program offers four-day trips between July and September. Walk noisily through Kodiak's backcountry to reduce the chances of confrontations with bears. During the salmon season, bears appear along the streams and beaches.

Kotzebue

A large, predominantly Eskimo community, served by daily jet from Anchorage and Fairbanks, Kotzebue is the headquarters for

NANA, one of the regional Native corporations that was established in 1971 with the passage of the Alaska Native Claims Settlement Act, which granted Alaskan Natives nearly $1 billion and title to 44 million acres (18 million hectares) of land. The money and the ground were divided up by 13 Native corporations: NANA's share was significant and it is now one of the more successful of the corporations. NANA is also actively involved in the reindeer industry and is a significant economic force in western Alaska.

MUSEUM OF THE ARCTIC

Tours of the NANA-run museum include a one-and-a-half-hour program unequaled anywhere in Alaska. It includes story

Above: *sea otters taking a bath*

telling, traditional Inupiat dancing and an award-winning slide show. The museum's exhibits include artifacts and traditional art and examples of all the animals indigenous to the region. It is a splendid introduction to the land and its traditional Native culture. The package also includes a city tour, a visit to the National Park Service office to learn about the wildlife and wilderness areas, and a culture camp demonstration which explains Native culture from both the spiritual and the practical perspectives. Guides take visitors on a walk in the tundra to point out permafrost as well as plants and their traditional uses.

Mendenhall Glacier

Some 13 miles (21 km) north of Juneau, a US Forest Service Information Center sits on the edge of a frigid lake into which Mendenhall Glacier calves icebergs large and small. The face of the glacier is about 1 mile (2 km) away, while its 1,500 sq. miles (3,880 sq. km) of ice and snow is called the Juneau Icefield. The most exciting way to savor the glacier and icefield is to take a trip organized by an air charter companies, or one of the helicopter carriers that fly over the great white deserts of snow and land on the surface of the icefield.

Above: *a helicopter hovers over a glacier*

Misty Fjords National Monument

Misty Fjords is a designated national wilderness as well as a national monument, and within the 3,570 sq. miles (9,240 sq. km) of its largely untouched coast and backcountry lie three major rivers, hundreds of small streams and creeks, icefields, glaciers, snowcapped mountains and mountain-top lakes. The great glaciers – thousands of feet deep – that filled Southeast Alaksa's bays and valleys slowly ground their way seaward from mountain-top heights. In the process they carved and scoured great steep-walled cliffs that now plunge from mountain summits to considerable depths below sea level. The effect of this has never been more beautifully evident than it is in Misty Fjords.

This 2.2 million-acre (890,000-hectare) wilderness is the southernmost of Alaska's 18 national monuments. There are tiny coves, great bays, and forest groves so thick you can barely see daylight through them. Wildlife includes brown and black bears, Sitka black-tail deer, wolves, mountain goats, beavers, mink,

Above: iceberg in Mendenhall Glacier lake

marten, foxes and river otters. But it is not only a place of scenery and wildlife on a grand scale: it also has tremendous commercial value as some of Alaska's most productive fish-rearing streams are located here.

There are very few marks of human activity inside the Misty Fjords area, and no roads leading to it; you can get there only by water or by air. Some travelers opt for a combination cruise/fly tour – going in by water and out by air, or vice versa. Some cruise-ships visit the monument as part of an Inside Passage trip (see page 55). You can fly there with one of several Ketchikan air charter companies, cruise there by charter boat or sign on with an outfit called Alaska Cruises and take one of the daily summer-time yacht tours.

Mount McKinley

Alaskan Indians called the mountain *Denali,* "The Great One," and although in later years it was officially designated Mount McKinley by the US Government, the old name is still used by Natives and locals. McKinley is part of the Alaska Range, a 600-mile (960-km) arc of mountains stretching across the southeast quarter of the state. It is the most spectacular mountain in North America. At 20,320 ft (6,195 meters), it is also the highest. It could be called the

Right: *a fisherman's idyll*

highest in the world, as its north face rises almost 18,000 ft (5,500 meters) above its base, an elevation gain that surpasses Mount Everest. The mountain is surrounded by one of the world's greatest wildlife sanctuaries – Denali National Park *(see pages 32–33)*. *www.denaliguide.com*

Mount St Elias

Mount St Elias is one of the North American continent's 10 highest peaks (18,010 ft/5,490 meters). It is part of the St Elias range, one of four major mountain ranges in the Wrangell-St Elias National Park *(see page 64–65)*. *www.nps.gov/wrst*

Nome

It was gold, discovered in 1898, that brought people to this windswept, wave-battered beach on the Seward Peninsula, 75 miles (120 km) or more from the nearest tree. Nome is still very much a frontier town. The beach is still open to the public: anyone with

Above: majestic Mount McKinley

a gold pan or a sluice box can search for gold along the waterfront, and camping is permitted, too.

There's not a lot else to do in Nome, unless you time your arrival to coincide with one of their enthusiastic celebrations, of which the Midnight Sun Festival and the Iditarod Trail Sled Dog Race are the biggest *(see page 70)*.

North Pole

Just outside Fairbanks the North Pole is the home of Santa Claus. Urban renewal forced Santa to move closer to the highway, where he poses year-round for pictures at Santaland, a thriving commercial enterprise on the Richardson Highway. The North Pole is home to 1,500 people and a surrounding population of 13,000. It has its own utilities, shopping malls and a large MAPCO petrol refinery.

Panhandle (Inside Passage)

The sights along the Inside Passage are surprisingly varied: there are two capital cities along its length, one Canadian and one American; and there are tiny Native villages where the food on most tables still depends on the harvest of sea, land and forest and the skills of the hunters and fishermen.

There are condos and high-rise hotels as modern as can be found in any of the communities of the world, and there are tiny, hand-built cabins and camps in isolated wilderness settings.

Above: Nome River

But there is this commonality all along the way: lush green forests of hemlock, cedar and fir cover whole islands and mountains except for snow-capped peaks and gravel beaches. Generous bays and exquisite little coves vie for attention; rivers course through glacier-carved valleys, while waterfalls plunge from mountainside cliffs to the sea.

The islands afford protection and nurture for a wide variety of wild creatures. Sitka black-tail deer are numerous; humpback and killer whales, porpoises and sea lions are frequent sights. Eagles are everywhere, diving and swooping to grab unwary fish; and there are huge black ravens, tiny gray wrens and black-capped Arctic terns, plus hundreds of different waterfowl – and the fishing here is world-class.

AMERICAN BALD EAGLE NATURAL HISTORY MUSEUM

In late fall the world's greatest gathering of bald eagles – more than 3,000 of them, many coming from hundreds of miles away – flies to a nearby river to feast on a late run of salmon in ice-free waters. The museum, on the Haines Highway, has a fascinating diorama.

HAINES

Eighty air miles (130 km) north of Juneau, Haines is rich in Tlingit Native culture and is best known for its majestic mountain scenery, king and sockeye salmon-fishing, and bald-headed eagles.

Old Fort William Henry Seward to the south of town has mas-

Above: a haughty bald eagle

sive early 20th-century officers' homes and command buildings still surrounding the old rectangular grounds.

The Alaska Indian Arts Center, a totem pole carving studio open for public viewing is located here. The Chilkat Center for Performing Arts nearby (open Mon–Sat 9am–12 noon, 1–5pm) stages dance productions throughout the summer months.

JUNEAU

The state capital is a port-of-call for every cruise-ship, ferry and airline that comes to southeast Alaska *(see separate entry, page 38).*

KETCHIKAN

Ketchikan is famous for four things: totem poles (more historic poles than anywhere else in the world – guided tours at the Totem Heritage Center); salmon (caught in considerable numbers both by

Above: *Chilkat dancers in Haines*

sport and commercial fishermen) – cross Ketchikan Creek to the Deer Mountain Tribal Hatchery); as the jumping-off place for Misty Fjords National Monument *(see page 52)*; and finally, as one of the few places where a brothel has been turned into a museum (Dolly's House provides an interesting insight into one important, if not much discussed, aspect of frontier life).*www.visit-ketchikan.com*

PETERSBURG
Just a few minutes by plane from Wrangell, Petersburg is bypassed by most tour ships, yet this spick-and-span little community of Norwegian descendants has much to offer visitors who enjoy poking around on their own. There are ancient Native Alaskan petroglyphs on the beaches when the tide is low, and the small but tasteful Clausen Memorial Museum offers insight into the history and art of fishing. Simply wandering the docks and wharves of the community will give the visitor a view of the large halibut fishing fleet. *www.petersburg.org*

Above: Little Norway festival in Petersburg

SITKA

In 1799 the Russian trader and colonizer Alexander Baranof established his headquarters in Sitka. Actually, Tlingit Natives had been there centuries before, and near the site of present-day Sitka two of the bloodiest battles between Alaska Natives and Russian colonists were fought. Today, the city is a pleasurable blend of Tlingit, Russian and American culture. The Russian Orthodox Cathedral of St Michael, with its priceless icons and other religious treasures, is reason enough to visit this city. Another good reason is the Sitka National Historical Park. Besides an excellent collection of totem poles, there is a museum about the battle fought on this site and a workshop where you can see Tlingit artisans at work.

Nearby, a conducted tour of the Alaska Raptor Rehabilitation Center is the highlight for many people. Bald eagles and other birds of prey recuperate here before being released into the wild. *www.sitka.com*

SKAGWAY

The northernmost of all the communities usually visited on a tour of the Inside Passage *(see pages 55–56). www.skagway.org*

WRANGELL

A small, untouristy patch of authentic Alaska, Wrangell is bypassed by most cruise-boats and visitors. This is a pity, because it is

Right: *Fourth of July celebrations*

a small untouristy patch of authentic Alaska. The fishing is excellent, and the people are friendly. There is an interesting museum and an easily accessible totem park and community house on Chief Shakes Island. Wrangell is also known for its ancient rock carvings, which can be seen at low tide at the north end of town. A boat trip up the nearby Stikine River is a voyage back into the past. *www.wrangell.com*

Pribilof Islands

Three hundred miles (480 km) off the western coast of Alaska lie the Pribilofs, the nesting grounds for hundreds of thousands of sea birds of 200 different species, and the breeding grounds and summer home of Pacific fur seals. There's a small hotel in St Paul (population about 700) and two small restaurants. Scheduled air service is available from Anchorage to St Paul, and there are package tours – the easiest way to visit the islands.

Above: fishing boats in Wrangell harbour

Prince William Sound

The Sound's wonderful natural displays of animals, ice, forest and mountains rarely disappoint visitors, but if you are thinking of making a visit, remember that it rains a lot. Here, where coastal peaks form a cloud-stopping arc from Whittier to Cordova, precipitation is measured in feet, not inches. Much of that moisture, driven into the Sound by the Gulf of Alaska's wicked winter storms, pours onto maritime rainforests.

Even more precipitation falls as snow and adds substance to the Sound's numerous glaciers. Come summer, moisture, too thick to be called fog, hangs between gray-green glassy salt water and clouds the color of concrete.

You can savor the atmosphere of Prince William Sound simply by crossing it on a ferry or tour boat. But if you take a trip down the Sound between Whittier and Valdez, some of the most interesting sights you will see – along with the humpback and killer whales, Dall porpoises, sea lions and harbor seals – are:

COLUMBUS GLACIER

The largest of the many glaciers that drop down into the northerly fjords of the Sound. It flows more than 40 miles (65 km) from the mountains to Columbia Bay, where its 4-mile (6.5-km) wide face daily drops hundreds of thousands of tons of ice into the sound. So much ice has filled the bay in recent years that boats can't approach the glacier as closely as they could in the past.

Above: *sea lions in Prince William Sound*

COPPER RIVER HIGHWAY

The highway traces the railroad line across the biologically rich Copper River Delta to Child's Glacier. The delta is a bird-watcher's paradise, home to the world's entire nesting population of dusky Canada geese and swarms of migrating waterfowl.

CORDOVA

An attractive community of wood-framed houses, Cordova was born a railroad town with the arrival of men in search of copper in 1906. The town can't be reached by road: Whittier-Valdez ferries stop here; otherwise it is reached by a short flight from Anchorage. The Small Boat Harbor is a lively spot and there's the Cordova Historical Museum, with historical and marine exhibits. There's a marvelous view of the town and the Sound from the Mount Eyak Ski area.

VALDEZ

Situated to the east of the 1964 earthquake epicenter *(see pages 18–19)*, Valdez was completely destroyed, and rebuilt on a different site. Consequently there are no buildings of historic interest, but Valdez is a lively town, which grew to prosperity as the terminus of the trans-Alaska pipeline, and its setting is splendid. The Valdez Museum and Historical Archive has a variety of exhibits, including one on the *Exxon Valdez* oil spill. *www.valdezalaska.org*

Above: *under sail in the Sound*

Skagway

There's nowhere in Alaska quite like Skagway when it comes to blending history with natural beauty. Situated at the northern end of the Inside Passage, Skagway is the natural jumping-off point for the shortcut over the coastal mountains into Canada's Yukon. This was a gold rush town, founded in 1897, and it trades on its lively past. The center of activity is along Broadway, where more than 60 gold rush-era buildings still stand. The Klondike Gold Rush National Historic Park has spent millions of dollars on their restoration and private efforts have also breathed life into old structures.

ARCTIC BROTHERHOOD HALL

The exterior of Brotherhood Hall is covered with thousands of pieces of driftwood. The interior is the home of the informative Trail of '98 Historical Museum, full of gold rush memorabilia.

Above: wood-framed houses in Cordova

EAGLE'S HALL

An historical melodrama – "Skagway in the Days of '98" – follows an hour of live ragtime music and gambling. The dealers are cast members, the money is phoney, and some of the tables date back to the gold rush. The show's popularity has kept it going since 1925.

KLONDIKE GOLD RUSH NATIONAL PARK CENTER

The center offers informative talks, an atmospheric movie about the gold rush days, and free walking tours of the historic district.

MASCOT SALOON

Built in 1898, the Mascot Saloon has some well-displayed exhibits that conjure up the tough atmosphere of the town's heyday.

Wrangell-St Elias National Park

America's largest park, at 13.2 million acres (5.3 million hectares), was "discovered" by visitors in the late 1980s. Before visiting, stop off at the headquarters at Glennallen, 200 miles

(320 km) east of Anchorage, for details. The northern entry to the park is the unpaved, 45-mile (72-km) Nabesna Road. It is suitable for 2-wheel-drive vehicles, but motorists are advised to check road conditions beforehand, as sections are occasionally washed out during summer rainstorms. Caribou, moose and grizzlies may be spotted in the open countryside bordering Nabesna Road, and large populations of Dall sheep are found in the hills surrounding the 9,358-ft (2,850-meter) Tanada Peak.

The principal road into the park is McCarthy Road; 60 miles (95 km) long and unpaved, it stretches all the way from Chitina at the western boundary to the gateway community of McCarthy. At its doorstep are rugged peaks that rise above raging rivers, fed by massive glaciers. There are half- or full-day hikes from McCarthy to nearby Kennicott Glacier and Root Glacier; and the historic, abandoned Kennicott copper-mining camp is only 4 miles (7 km) away.

The Skolai Creek-Chitistone River area is the most popular of the backcountry destinations. The Ahtnas, an Athabascan tribe, used to use this route for hunting and trading.

The Skookum Volcanic Trail (Mile 38 of the Nabesna Road) leads to a tundra area with volcanic dikes and basalt flows and is ideal for day hikers. *www.nps.gov/wrst*

Left: Skagway transport **Above:** solitude in Wrangell National Park

ESSENTIAL INFORMATION

The Place

Capital: Juneau.

Area: 586,000 sq. miles (1,430,000 sq. km).

Population: 621,400, of which 42 percent live in the Anchorage area. There is a population of some 104,100 indigenous people, about half of whom are Eskimos.

Religion: A mixture of all religions that are represented in the rest of the United States, plus a strong Russian Orthodox influence in the south.

Time Zone: Alaska Standard Time (Pacific Standard Time minus 1 hour; Eastern Standard Time minus 5 hours; GMT minus 10 hours). The Aleutian Chain and St Lawrence Island are in the Hawaii-Aleutian Time Zone, which is 1 hour earlier.

Dialing Code: US international code (1) + 907.

Weights and Measures: Imperial.

Electricity: 110/120 volts.

Highest mountain: Mount McKinley (20,320 ft/6,196 meters).

Northernmost point: Point Barrow.

Largest lake: Lake Iliamna (1,100 sq. miles/2,850 sq. km).

Climate

Alaska's vastness defies attempts to categorize its climate. For convenience, however, the state can be divided into five regions about which some generalizations can be made.

Southeast: Wet and mild; certain communities in the region can receive more than 200 inches (5 meters) of precipitation annually. On rare, sunny days in summer, high temperatures might

Left: totem poles are one of the most dramatic forms of Native art

reach the mid-70°F (21°C) range. Winter temperatures rarely fall much below freezing.

Southcentral: Coastal communities are frequently as wet as southeastern cities, but rainfall lessens considerably just a short distance inland. Anchorage has had summer highs over 80°F (26°C) but the 60s (15–20°C) and low 70s (21–26°C) are more common.

Interior: Average 10 inches (25 cm) of moisture annually. Summer temperatures in the 70s and 80s (21–28°C) are common. Typical winter lows are to –40°F (–40°C).

Arctic Coast: High winds are common, along with low rainfall. Near Nome, summer temperatures in the high 30s (3°C) and 40s (4°C) are usual. Winter temperatures, though extreme, are never as low as in the Interior.

Southwest and The Aleutians: Some of the most miserable weather on earth. High winds can rise without warning and smash through the islands at 100 mph (160 km/h). Heavy fog is common.

Above: in Alaska's temperatures you don't want to capsize

Government and economy

In 1867 the US purchased Alaska from Russia for $7.2 million Threafter it was governed at different times by the US Army, the US Treasury Department and the US Navy. Finally, in 1884, the federal government declared the territory the District of Alaska, and a civil government was appointed. The discovery of oil on the Kenai Peninsula in 1957 dispelled the image of Alaska as a weak, dependent region, and on January 3, 1959, it became the 49th state. Juneau, the territorial capital, continued as the state capital.

Today, every dollar that flows through Alaska's economy originates from its land or water. The oil and mining industries extract vast wealth from under the ground, fishermen harvest much of the nation's seafood from the water, and loggers and tourism operators exploit the landscape itself. Natural resources are the real reason the economy, and the people it employs, are here at all.

Oil is by far the largest of Alaska's industries, but fishing is second and employs more people. Tourism also is a large employer. The logging industry is shrinking under the pressure of environmental concerns. The government employs more people than any other industry, and it is funded largely by oil revenues. Alaska's resource storehouse is vast, covering 365 million acres (148 million hectares) and only a fraction of 1 percent is privately owned. The federal government controls more than half, and the state government about a third.

Right: *fishing is the second-biggest industry*

Public Holidays

January 1 New Year's Day; **January 15** Martin Luther King's Birthday; **February (3rd Monday)** President's Day; **March (last Monday)** Seward's Day; **July 4** Independence Day; **September (1st Monday)** Labor Day; **October (3rd Monday)** Alaska Day; **November (2nd Monday)** Veterans' Day; **November (4th Thursday)** Thanksgiving; **December 25** Christmas

Festivals

Alaska celebrates a number of festivals. The major ones are:
Fur Rendezvous, Anchorage. Begins on the second Friday in February and lasts 10 days with more than 150 events. A highlight of the event is the World Championship Sprint Sled Dog Race.
Iditarod Trail Sled Dog Race. Starts from Anchorage on the first Saturday in March and covers more than 1,100 miles (1,770 km) to Nome.

Above: *blanket toss at the Fur Rendezvous*

Midnight Sun Run, June 21, part of Fairbanks's Summer Solstice Festival

Summer Solstice. Alaska's pleasure at the return of summer is celebrated statewide.

World Eskimo-Indian Olympics are held in Fairbanks in July. Twenty-five unconventional events requiring strength, speed, and endurance.

Getting there

BY AIR

International air carriers offering passenger service to Anchorage include: British Airways, Alaska Airlines and Aeroflot. In summer, there are numerous charter flights from a variety of European countries.

American domestic passenger carriers providing service from the Lower 48 states are Alaska Airlines, Continental, Delta, Reno Air, Northwest and United. Connections from Seattle are available for Ketchikan, Sitka, Wrangell, Juneau, Cordova and Fairbanks.

BY SEA

Many visitors arrive in Alaska via cruise-ship, a luxurious and exciting way to come. Cruise-ships sail through the spectacular Inside Passage arriving at Skagway, Ketchikan, Sitka, Juneau, Misty Fjord, Valdez, Seward and Anchorage. Around a dozen

Above: *landing on Lake Hood*

cruise lines serve Alaska, with several small vessels offering excursions. Cruises normally start from Vancouver, BC and San Francisco, with a few voyages leaving Seattle. Cruise lines normally operate between May and September and offer a variety of options including round-trip or one-way cruises.

Popular cruise lines serving Alaska include Cunard Line, Princess Cruises, Royal Caribbean Line and Westours/Holland America Line. For further information and to make reservations, contact a travel agent.

BY RAIL

There is no rail service directly to Alaska from the Lower 48, but the Alaska Railroad provides passenger services within the state. It connects Anchorage with Fairbanks to the north and with Whittier and Seward to the south.

For more information, contact Alaska Railroad, PO Box 1-07500, Anchorage, Alaska 99510-7500; tel: 907-265-2494 or toll-free 800-544-0552.

Entry requirements

For non-US citizens, the same entry requirements apply as for the rest of the United States – a valid passport and in some cases a visa. Visitors from the UK do not normally need a visa if staying for less than 90 days.

Above: the road to Eureka Summit

Planning the trip

The Alaska State Division of Tourism publishes annually the *Alaska Vacation Planner*. It is a booklet crammed with facts about Alaska and a directory of where to stay, eat and tour. This office should be able to point you in the right direction if you want a customized holiday, whether it is a cruise, a wilderness adventure, a kayaking holiday or a fishing tour.

There is a free state-published booklet on the Alaska highway system which can be obtained from the same address.

To obtain a free copy of either booklet, write to the Alaska Division of Tourism, PO Box 110801, Juneau, Alaska 99811, tel: 907-465-2012; fax: 907-465-5442; *www.dced.state.ak.us/tourism/*

Health

Two major hospitals serve the general public in Anchorage, in Fairbanks and Juneau. They also provide 24-hour emergency service; treatment is thorough and professional. Hospital costs in Alaska, as all over the US, are very high and visitors should take out comprehensive private insurance before their trip.

Security and Crime

Alaska is not crime-ridden, but occasional outbursts of violence are not unknown. Use basic common sense as you would anywhere else. Sexual assault rates are quite high and women should not

Right: *a sternwheeler always attracts passengers*

travel alone in secluded areas (such as wooded bike paths), near bars or other potentially troublesome areas.

Leave large amounts of money, travelers' checks, jewelry and other valuables in the hotel safe. Don't overtly display valuables and be careful where you leave packages and bags.

Money

Travelers' checks in US dollars are advisable. National banks in Alaska's major cities – Anchorage, Fairbanks and Juneau – can convert foreign currency at the prevailing exchange rate. Outside these areas it can be difficult. Automatic Teller Machines (ATMs) can be found in just about every town on the road system.

There is no state sales tax in Alaska, but different boroughs may impose a sales tax on some or all goods and services.

Media

PRINT

Three major daily newspapers are published: the *Juneau Empire,* the *Anchorage Daily News* and the *Fairbanks Daily News-Miner*. Many smaller communities also put out newspapers and are not afraid to tackle important or controversial local issues. Bookstores

normally have one or more of the major dailies on sale. In large cities, Seattle newspapers, the *New York Times* and the *Wall Street Journal* are normally available. English and other foreign newspapers are very rarely available.

Left: *a friendly fisherwoman*

TELEVISION

Only Anchorage has enough stations to affiliate actively with the four major US television networks. These are CBS, Channel 11; ABC, Channel 13; NBC, Channel 2; and Fox Network, Channel 4. Other major cities will usually offer a spread of programs from the major networks along with a variety of locally produced shows.

The vast majority of programs are transmitted in English, although a number of regional shows may be broadcast in the area's Native dialect. Most of these programs are on public television.

RADIO

Some commercial radio stations in Alaska are still used to pass on messages to residents living in the bush. Regularly scheduled times are set aside for transmitting everything from messages of endearment to doctors' appointments.

The major radio networks have affiliates in all the larger cities, and most towns or villages of any consequence will have a locally owned radio station. Quality varies from excellent to terrible.

Above: a smart resort hotel

Accommodations

Accommodations in Alaska vary greatly. Larger communities offer a range of hotels, with luxury accommodations of an international standard available, as well as more homely places in which to stay. Bed-and-breakfasts are also very popular across the state, with many offering outstanding service along with a personal touch.

In the very smallest communities, facilities may be mediocre or non-existent. Regardless of where you stay, the prices are likely to seem high, especially during the summer months, when it is high season.

During 1997 and 1998, Anchorage experienced a boom in hotel construction, with new facilities built near the airport, downtown, midtown and on the east side. Many of the new hotels offer relatively lower rates but with few extras, such as full-service restaurants or conference facilities.

For information about bed-and-breakfast accommodations, write to Alaska Private Lodgings/Stay With A Friend, 704 W. 2nd Avenue, Anchorage, AK 99501, tel: (907) 258-1717.

The Alaska Division of Tourism can provide an extensive list of accommodations throughout the state published in the Alaska Vacation Planner, mentioned earlier. Contact Alaska Division of Tourism, PO Box 110801, Juneau, AK 99811, tel: (907) 465-2010.

Above: the float plane awaits **Right:** *cabin life*

FOREST SERVICE CABINS

Visitors can stay in remote wilderness cabins maintained by the US Forest Service or Alaska State Parks. The cabins are accessible by trails, boat or chartered air service (arranged by the renter). There are over 200 cabins scattered throughout the Tongass and Chugach National Forest in Southeast and Southcentral Alaska. They are located in beautiful, remote areas and give visitors a chance to experience the great outdoors on their own, but they are very basic. Averaging 12 x 14 ft (3.7 x 4.3 meters), they lack running water and electricity. They are equipped with a table and oil- or wood-burning stove for heat. Wooden bunks without mattresses are provided and outhouses are located a few steps away. Cabins on a lake often have an aluminum boat or skiff available.

Renters bring their own food, stoves, cooking utensils and bedding and replace any firewood they burn. Outfitters and air charter operators help with gear needed for a cabin stay. The cost of rentals is very reasonable but getting there can be quite expensive.

For more information on Forest Service cabins, write to the Alaska Public Lands Information Center, 605 W. Fourth Avenue,

Suite 105, Anchorage, AK 99501, tel: (907) 271-2599 or Tongass National Forest, Centennial Hall, 101 Egan Drive, Juneau, AK 99801, tel: (907) 586-8751.

CAMPGROUNDS

Federal, state, municipal and private campgrounds dot the landscape in Alaska. They can vary from barely organized tent sites to full hook-up recreational vehicle parking sites, with rates varying accordingly. They all operate during the summer months only. The best source of advance information is the Alaska State Division of Tourism, PO Box 110801, Juneau, AK 99811, tel: (907) 465-2010.

Useful Websites

www.travelalaska.com Official site of Alaska's tourist board; provides a trip planner, field reports and cultural information.
www.alaskan.com Links to national parks, accommodations, transportation, arts and crafts and outdoor adventure tours.
www.akrr.com Rail information for travel inside Alaska.
www.alaskaone.com Information on all areas of Alaska as well as transportation and accommodation details.
www.alaskanative.net Official page for the Alaska Native Heritage Center. Includes cultural and program information.

Above: *Fairbanks festival*

Also from Insight Guides…

Insight Guides is the award-winning classic series that provides the complete picture of a destination, with expert and informative text and the world's best photography. Each book has everything you need, being an ideal travel planner, a reliable on-the-spot guide, and a superb souvenir of a trip. Nearly 200 titles.

Insight Maps are designed to complement the guidebooks. They provide full, clear mapping of major destinations, list top sights, and their laminated finish makes them durable and easy to fold. More than 100 titles.

Insight Compact Guides are handy reference books, modestly priced but comprehensive. Text, pictures and maps are all cross-referenced, making them ideal books for on-the-spot use. 120 titles.

Insight Pocket Guides pioneered the concept of the authors as "local hosts" who provide personal recommendations, just as they would give honest advice to a friend. Pull-out map included. 120 titles.

The world's largest collection of visual travel guides

And now for the big picture...

The text you have been reading is extracted from *Insight Guide: Alaska*, one of more than 200 titles in the award-winning Insight Guides series. Its 350 pages are packed with expert essays covering Alaska's history and culture, detailed itineraries for the entire state, a comprehensive listings section, a full set of clear, cross-referenced maps, and hundreds of stunning photographs. It's an inspiring background read, an invaluable on-the-spot companion, and a superb souvenir of a visit. Available from all good bookshops.

INSIGHT GUIDES

The world's largest collection of visual travel guides